From Fruit to Jam

From Fruit to Jam

Ali Mitgutsch

Carolrhoda Books, Inc., Minneapolis

First published in the United States of America 1981 by
Carolrhoda Books, Inc.

Manufactured in the United States of America

LIBRARY OF CONGRESS CATALOGING IN PUBLICATION DATA

Mitgutsch, Ali.
From fruit to jam.

(A Carolrhoda start to finish book)
Edition for 1976 published under title: Vom Obst zur Marmelade.
SUMMARY: Describes how jam is made from fresh fruit.

1. Jam—Juvenile literature. [1. Jam] I. Title.

TX612.J3M5713 1981 641.8′52 81-58
ISBN 0-87614-154-8

2 3 4 5 6 7 8 9 10 86 85 84 83 82

From Fruit to Jam

In the summer we have lots of fresh, ripe fruit.

Near the ground, sweet strawberries turn red.

High in the trees, plums and peaches and cherries ripen.

We eat some of this fruit just as it is.

Some is canned to eat later.

And some is made into jellies and jams.

After the fruit has been picked, it is washed.
Then the stems, leaves, and skins are taken off.
If the fruit has seeds, they must be taken out too.
Now the fruit is ready to be made into jam.

The fruit is put into a large cooking pot.

Sugar is added to it.

Sugar makes the jam taste sweet.

It also helps keep the jam fresh for a long time.

As the fruit cooks,
juice runs out of it.
At first the juice is thin.
But as the sugar melts into it,
the juice gets thicker.

When the jam has thickened,
it is ready to be put into jars.
The jars must be very clean,
so they are first put into boiling water.
While they are still hot from being boiled,
the hot jam is poured into them.
When the jam cools, it will be thick and firm.

The jars must be sealed tightly to keep the jam fresh.
One way to seal the jars is with preserving skin.
Preserving skin is like cellophane.
It is cut to the right size
and smoothed over the top of the jar.
Then a clean lid is put on the jar.

The jam is stored in a dark, cool storeroom or cellar.
It will stay fresh for about three years.

In the summer we can eat fresh fruit.
The jam that is made from this fruit
can be eaten all year round.
Homemade jam tastes wonderful any time of year!

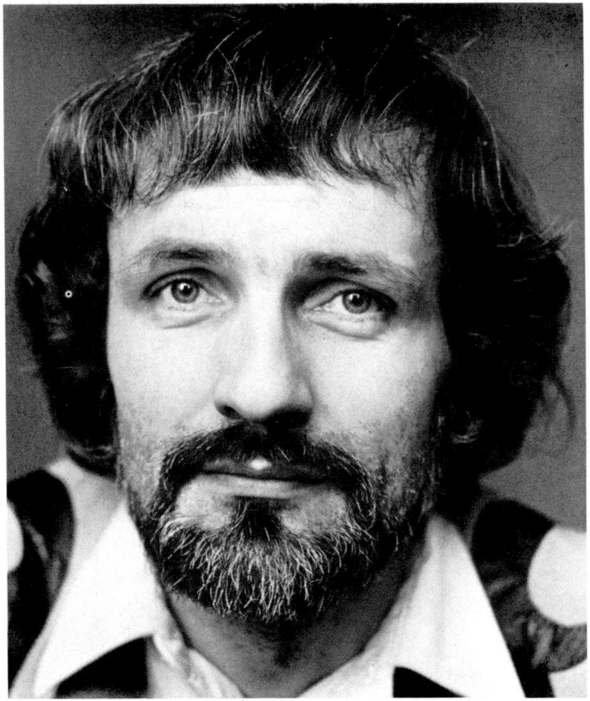

Ali
Mitgutsch

ALI MITGUTSCH is one of Germany's best-known children's book illustrators. He is a devoted world traveler, and many of his book ideas have taken shape during his travels. Perhaps this is why they have such international appeal. Mr. Mitgutsch's books have been published in 22 countries and are enjoyed by thousands of readers around the world.

Ali Mitgutsch lives with his wife and three children in Schwabing, the artists' quarter in Munich. The Mitgutsch family also enjoys spending time on their farm in the Bavarian countryside.

THE CAROLRHODA START TO FINISH BOOKS

From Beet to Sugar
From Blossom to Honey
From Cacao Bean to Chocolate
From Cement to Bridge
From Clay to Bricks
From Cotton to Pants
From Cow to Shoe
From Dinosaurs to Fossils
From Egg to Bird
From Egg to Butterfly
From Fruit to Jam
From Grain to Bread
From Grass to Butter
From Ice to Rain
From Milk to Ice Cream
From Oil to Gasoline
From Ore to Spoon
From Sand to Glass
From Seed to Pear
From Sheep to Scarf
From Tree to Table